At the Seaside

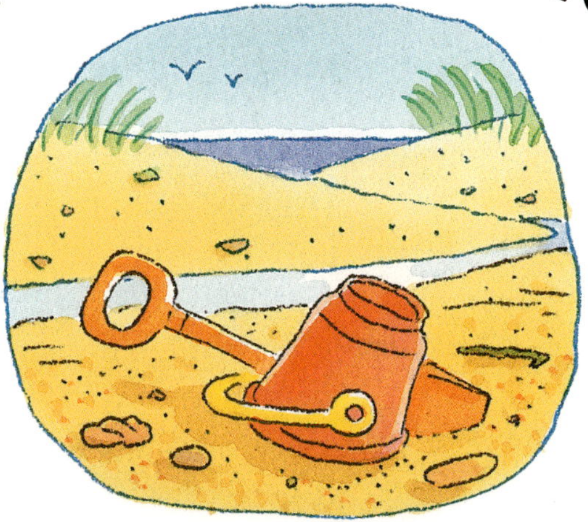

Moira Andrew
Illustrated by Clive Scruton

RIGBY

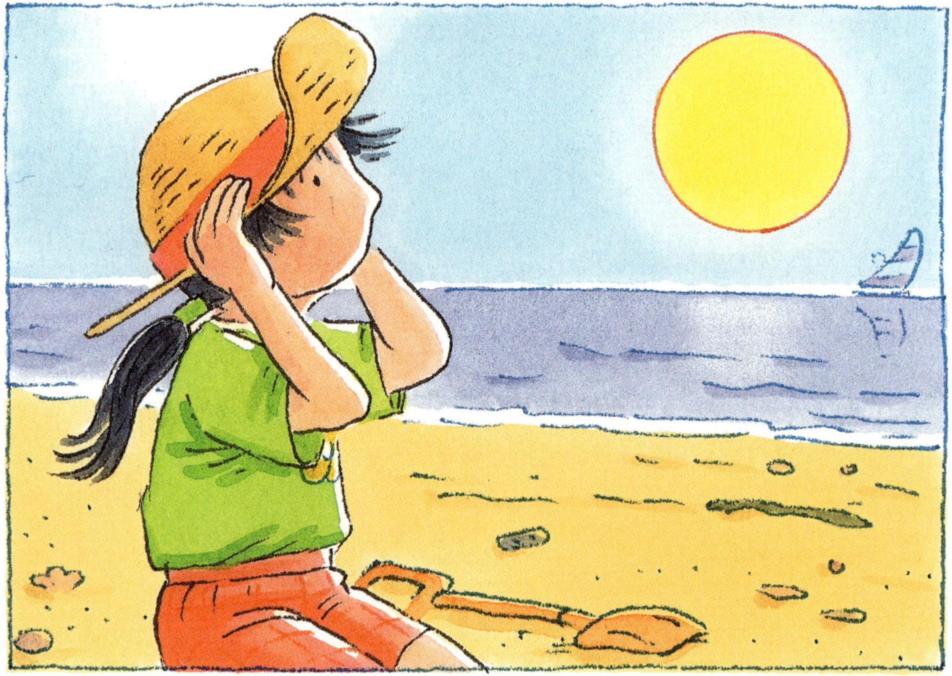

the sun

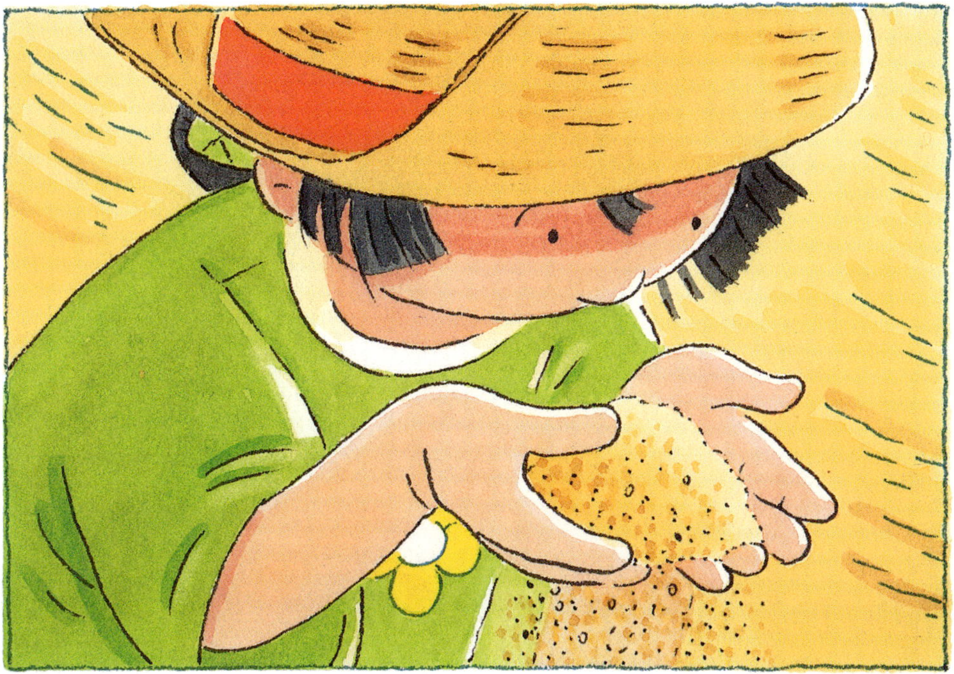

the sand

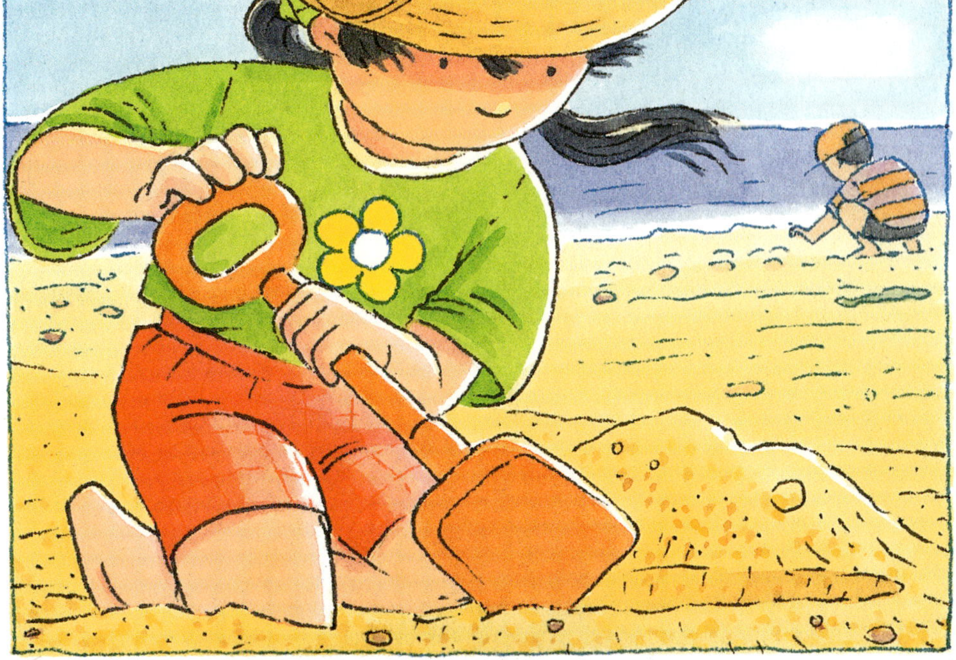

the spade

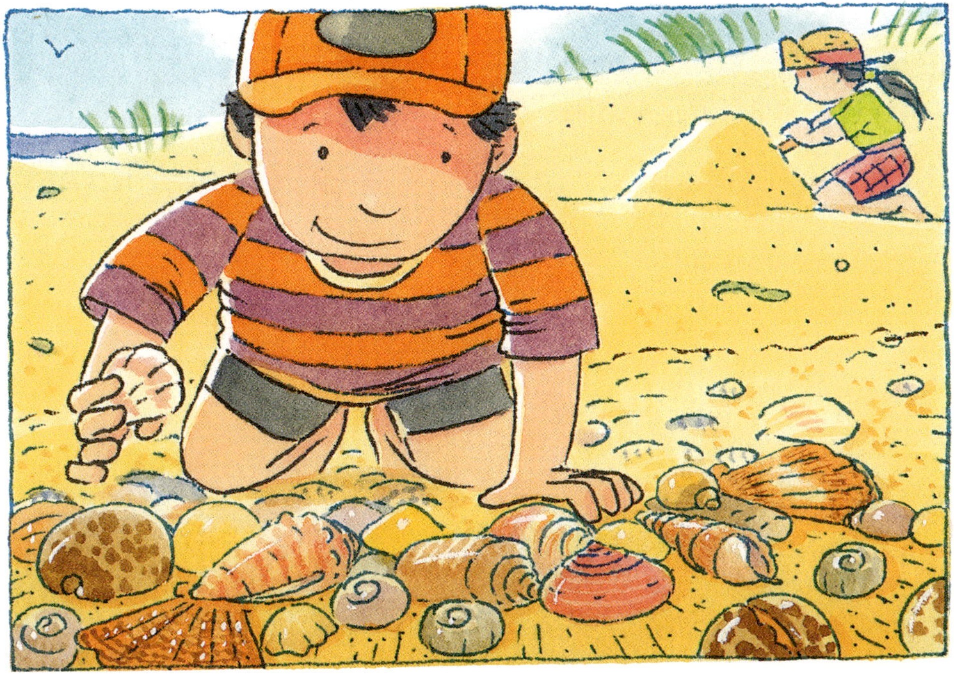

the shells

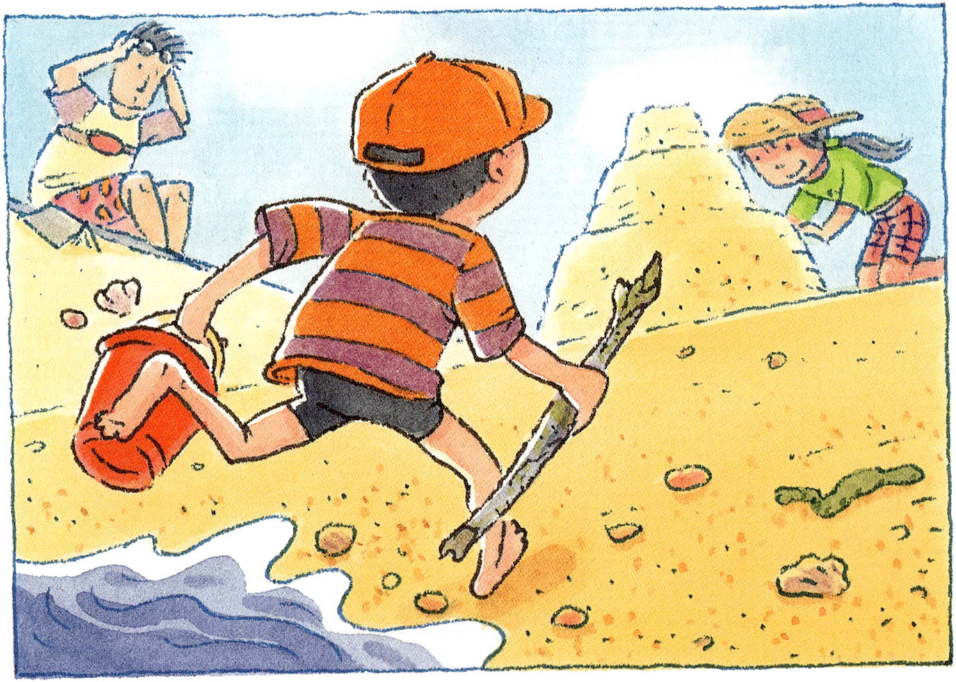

the stick

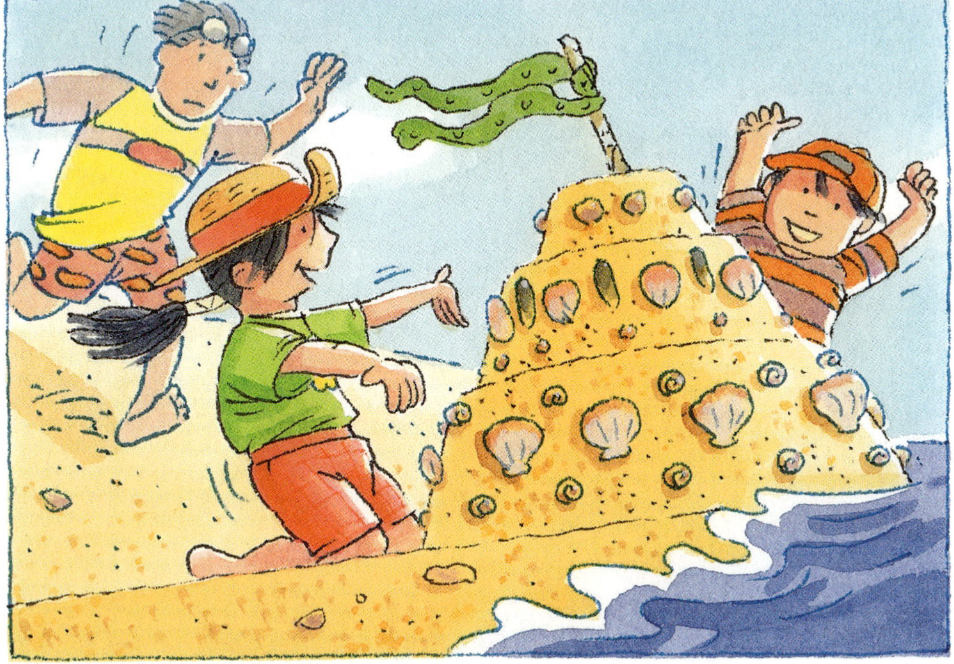

the sandcastle

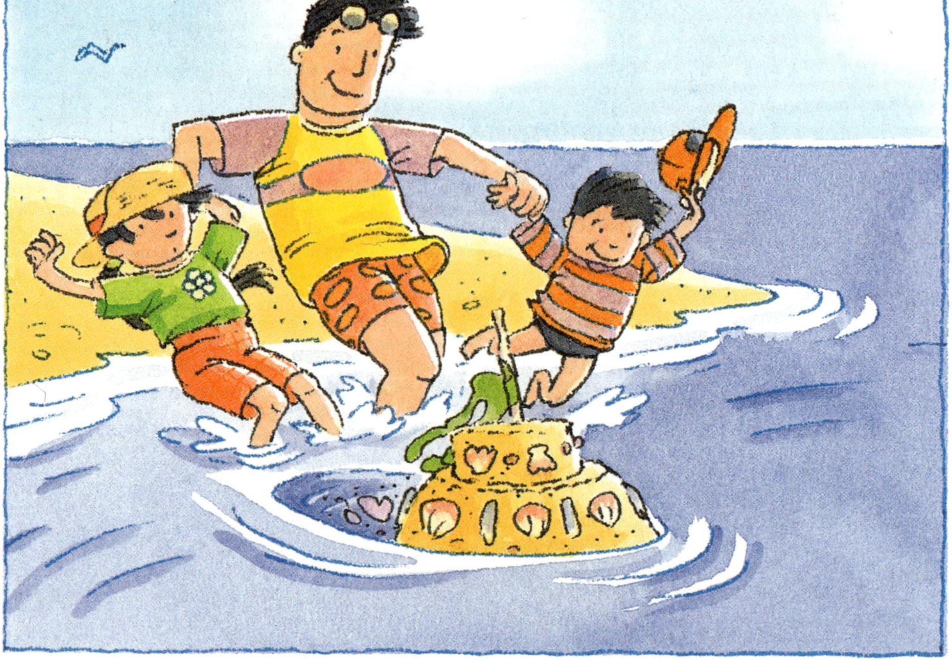

the sea